Temple Prime

Some Account of the Family of Prime, of Rowley, Mass

With notes on the Families of Platts and Jewett by Temple Prime

Temple Prime

Some Account of the Family of Prime, of Rowley, Mass
With notes on the Families of Platts and Jewett by Temple Prime

ISBN/EAN: 9783743413481

Manufactured in Europe, USA, Canada, Australia, Japa

Cover: Foto ©ninafisch / pixelio.de

Manufactured and distributed by brebook publishing software
(www.brebook.com)

Temple Prime

Some Account of the Family of Prime, of Rowley, Mass

SOME ACCOUNT OF

THE FAMILY OF

PRIME

OF ROWLEY, MASS.

WITH NOTES ON THE FAMILIES OF

PLATTS AND JEWETT

BY

TEMPLE PRIME

(HUNTINGTON, N. Y.)

Second Edition

NEW-YORK
1897

SOME ACCOUNT OF

THE FAMILY OF

PRIME

OF ROWLEY, MASS.

WITH NOTES ON THE FAMILIES OF

PLATTS AND JEWETT

BY

TEMPLE PRIME

(HUNTINGTON, N. Y.)

Second Edition

NEW-YORK
1897

PRIME.

MARK I PRIME.

Born: in England.

Died: Rowley,[1] Mass.; buried there, December 21st, 1683.

Married: Anne ——; died, Rowley; buried there, September 6th 1672.

Will: no date; proved April 15th 1684. Probate Office, Essex Co., Mass. Liber 4, fol. 76.[2]

Issue.

1. **Samuel I Prime,** of whom later.
2. **Mary Prime,** buried at Rowley, January 6th 1654–55.

Account of Mark I Prime.

Though his family was not among the 60 families that settled at Rowley in 1639, it is on record that, previous to January 1644–45, he had assigned to him a house-lot of 1½ acres adjoining the southerly side of William Acey's land (on Holmes Street) east end on the street; it was opposite Daniel J. Hale's house, and is now owned by Thomas P. Hale; the present house was built by Joshua I Prime.

---

[1] See page 32. [2] See page 32.

Mark I was probably a miller, as appears by an affidavit[1] taken by him June 23d 1656.

1654, Overseer.

1663 and 1664, judge of delinquents for not attending town-meetings.

1674, a voter on the minister's stipend.

SAMUEL I PRIME.

Born: Rowley, August 14th 1649.

Died: Rowley, March 18th 1683–84; buried there.

Will: intestate; Sarah his widow and Abel Platts were appointed administrators, April 15th 1684; they died, and were replaced March 31st 1695–96 by Samuel Platts; the estate was finally wound up with that of Mark I Prime, March 8th 1696–97.[2]

Married: January 1st 1673–74, Sarah, daughter of Samuel Platts[3] and of Sarah —— his wife; born, Rowley, October 16th 1654; her second husband was Capt. Moses Bradstreet of Ipswich, Mass.; she died before 1696.

Issue.

1. **Samuel II Prime,** of whom later.
2. **Sarah Prime,** born May 8th 1678; married June 25th 1733 James Stewart; she died December 29th 1747.
3. **Mark II Prime;** founder of the family still settled at Rowley.[4]
4. **Anne Prime,** born June 27th 1683; joined the church September 12th 1714, at that time unmarried.

---

[1] See page 36.
[2] See page 37.
[3] See page 68.
[4] See page 27.

NATHANIEL PRIME.

From a miniature in the possession of E. L. Coster, Esq.

SAMUEL II PRIME.

Born: Rowley, December 29th 1675.

Died: Rowley, March 4th 1717–18; buried there.[1]

Will: intestate; Sarah his widow, later the wife of Robert Rogers, having died, Moses Bradstreet was on the 10th of February 1722–23 appointed guardian of the children: Samuel Prime aged over 14, Joshua Prime aged under 14, Sarah Prime aged under 14; final settlement of the estate February 12th 1722–23.[2]

Married: (published March 23d 1705–06) Sarah, daughter of Joseph II Jewett[3] and of Ruth Wood his wife; born February 3d 1689–90; baptized February 10th, same year; married again, October 7th 1718 to Robert Rogers of Rowley; she died November 20th 1722.

Issue.

1. An infant, died January 14th 1706–07.
2. **Samuel III Prime,** born December 2d 1707; drowned September 30th 1730.[4]
3. **Mark III Prime,** born July 30th, 1710; died April 1717.[5]
4. **Joshua I Prime,** of whom later.
5. **Sarah Prime,** baptized February 5th 1715–16; married December 19th 1732 Josiah White of Wenham, Mass.
6. **Mark IV Prime,** posthumous; baptized March 23d 1717–18; died August 13th 1719.[5]

---

[1] His tombstone bears the following inscription:

HERE LYES Y^e BODY
OF SAMUEL PRIME
WHO DIED MARCH
Y^e 4th 1717–18 AGED
43 YEARS

[2] See page 45. [3] See page 72.

[4] In church register: "Poor Saml.".

[5] In church register: "A hopefull child."

Account of Samuel II Prime.

In 1708 he had permission given to him to erect for himself a pew in the meeting house at Rowley in the north corner in the gallery, and also one for his wife in the easterly corner of the gallery; besides the minister's pew, these were the first built.

JOSHUA I PRIME.

Born: Rowley, September 28th 1712.

Died: Sutton, Mass., July 26th 1770.

Will: intestate; his widow appointed administratrix, July 25th 1770. (Probate Office, Worcester co. Mass.)[1]

Married: 1st, Rowley, January 1st 1733–34 Mehetable daughter of Moses and Hannah Platts;[2] she was born, Rowley, November 11th 1712; died there October 17th 1751.

——— 2dly (published June 18th 1752), Bridget daughter of Nathaniel II Hammond and of Bridget —— his wife, of Ipswich (parish of Rowley): she married again at Sutton, Mass., December 29th 1772, by the Rev. David Hull to Nathaniel Carriel, Jr. of that place; she was dismissed, May 26th 1771, from the Rowley Church to that of Sutton, Mass.; alive in Sutton 1792.

Issue.

1. **Samuel IV Prime,** baptized, Rowley, August 18th 1734; died March 29th 1736.
2. **Joshua II Prime,** baptized, Rowley, December 14th 1735; died September 6th 1743.
3. **Sarah Prime,** baptized, Rowley, July 31st 1737; died March 12th 1749.

---

[1] See page 46. [2] See page 68.

CORNELIA SANDS,
MRS. NATHANIEL PRIME.

From a miniature in the possession of E. L. Coster, Esq.

4. **Samuel V Prime,** baptized, Rowley, 1740; alive in 1772.

5. **Moses Prime,** baptized, Rowley, September 19th 1742; died December 14th 1756.

6. **Joshua III Prime,** baptized, Rowley, October 14th 1744; died November 12th 1746.

7. **Joshua IV Prime,** baptized, Rowley, September 20th, 1747; died November 2d 1748.

8. **Josiah Prime,** baptized, Rowley, July 22d 1753; settled at Swausey, N. H.; married, Sutton, February 20th 1780 Rothiel Carriel; married again, Sutton, January 18th 1787 Hannah ——.

9. **Mehetable Prime,** born August 29th 1755; baptized, Rowley, September 3d of same year; married, Sutton, February 16th 1773 Isaiah Hammond of Swansey, N. H.

10. **Bridget Prime,** baptized, Rowley, September 11th 1757; died August 29th 1759.

11. **Joshua Jewett Prime,** born November 14th 1760; alive in 1772.

12. **Bridget Prime,** baptized, Rowley, November 21st 1762; married, Sutton, February 24th 1785 Seth Carpenter of Sutton.

13. **Oliver Prime,** baptized, Rowley, November 18th 1764; alive in 1772.

14. **Nathaniel I Prime,** of whom later.

15. **Abigail Prime,** born, Sutton, September 13th 1770; married, Sutton, January 14th 1790 Nathan Woodbury of Sutton.

Account of Joshua I Prime.

In 1753 he built a house at Rowley (at the present time owned by Thos. P. Hale) on the land assigned 1644 to Mark I Prime; he moved to Sutton, Mass. prior to 1770, and lived there on the land owned (1878) by Samuel Prescott and situated in District No. 11.

May 31st 1757 corporal in Capt. John Pearson's troop of horse at Rowley.

NATHANIEL I PRIME.

Born: Rowley, January 30th 1768; baptized there the next day; he was born in the house his father erected (1753) on the land assigned (1644) to Mark I Prime.

Died: N. Y. November 26th 1840; buried in his vault in the churchyard of St. Mark's-in-the-Bowery, N. Y.; remains removed in 1845 to vault in the churchyard of St. Paul's, Eastchester, N. Y.

Will: N. Y. April 24th 1840; proved December 23d 1840; Surrogate's Office N. Y., Liber 81, fol. 691.

Married: N. Y. June 3d 1797 by the Rev. Dr. Lynn of —— to Cornelia daughter of Comfort Sands and of Sarah Dodge his wife; she was born N. Y. November 8th 1773; died at the residence of her son Edward I Prime, 17 West 16th Street, N. Y. at 8:30 P. M. April 21st 1852; interred at Eastchester with her husband; will, N. Y. January 7th 1848, proved June 3d 1852; Surrogate's Office N. Y. Liber 104, fol. 137.

Issue.

1. **Emily Frances Prime**, born N. Y. December 25th 1798; died June 8th 1804; buried in Comfort Sands' vault, N. Y.; remains removed 1845 to Comfort Sands' vault at Eastchester.

2. **Cornelia I Prime**, born No. 146 Washington Street, N. Y., January 4th 1800; married N. Y. November 25th 1819 to Robert, son of Cornelius Ray of N. Y.; she died N. Y. May 21st 1874; interred in Greenwood Cemetery.

3. **Edward I Prime**, of whom later.

4. **Emily I Prime**, born 42 (now 54) Wall Street, N. Y., June 26th 1804; married N. Y. July 17th 1832 by the Rector of Grace Parish and by the Rev. Mr. Varela, to William Seton of N. Y.; she died, Pau, France, November 28th 1854; buried there.

5. **Rufus Prime**, of whom later.

6. **Frederick I Prime**, of whom later.

CORNELIA SANDS,
MRS. NATHANIEL PRIME.

7. **Matilda Prime,** born No. 1 Broadway, N. Y. July 2d 1810; baptized Grace Church, N. Y. February 27th 1811; married N. Y. June 9th 1831 by the Rector of Grace Parish to Gerard H. son of John G. Coster of N. Y.; she died, Paris, France, April 19th 1849; interred in Greenwood Cemetery.

8. **Laura Prime,** born, No. 1 Broadway, N. Y., February 17th 1812; married, N. Y., November 8th 1831 by the Rector of Grace Parish to John Clarkson, son of Peter A. Jay of N. Y.; died at Rye, July 30th 1888; services Christ Church, Rye, August 1st; buried in the Jay graveyard, Rye.

9. **Harriet I Prime,** born, No. 1 Broadway, N. Y., April 7th 1814; died, N. Y., March 24th 1824; interred in her father's vault at St. Mark's-in-the-Bowery; remains removed in 1845 to Eastchester.

EDWARD I PRIME AND HIS FAMILY.

Born: No. 42 (now 54) Wall Street, N. Y., December 10th 1801.

Died: Riverdale-on-Hudson, N. Y., Tuesday August 21st 1883; funeral at Christ Church, Riverdale; interred in Greenwood Cemetery.

Will: N. Y., February 27th 1879; proved September 24th 1883; Surrogate's Office N. Y., Liber 319, fol. 225.

Married: 1st, Hyde Park, Dutchess co., N. Y., September 18th 1827 by the Rev. Mr. Johnson to Anne, daughter of William Bard; she died, N. Y., October 27th 1834, in her 31st year; interred in Greenwood Cemetery.

——— 2dly, Westfarms, Westchester co., N. Y., May 20th 1836 by the Rector of St. Peter's Parish, to Charlotte Wilkins, daughter of William Hoffman, M. D. of Westfarms; she died, N. Y., May 29th 1892, in her 85th year; services Grace Church, N. Y., June 1st; buried at Greenwood.

Issue.

1. **Cornelia II Prime,** born, N. Y., February 6th 1829; baptized by the Rector of Grace Parish; married by the Rector of Grace Parish, January 26th 1850 to August Ahrens of N. Y.

2. **Nathaniel II Prime,** born, N. Y., July 23d 1830; baptized by the Rev. George L. Hinton, Harlem, N. Y., served in the U. S. army; died, N. Y., July 8th 1885; funeral at the Church of the Transfiguration, N. Y., July 10th; interred in Greenwood Cemetery; will, N. Y., October 27th 1883; proved October 6th 1885; Surrogate's Office N. Y. Liber 349, fol. 426.

3. **William Bard Prime,** born, N. Y., January 19th 1832; baptized in Grace Church; died September 8th 1836.

4. **Edward II Prime,** born, N. Y., October 19th 1833; baptized in Grace Church; married, December 3d 1889, by the Rector of Christ Church, Riverdale-on-Hudson, to Anne Rhodes, widow of William Hoffman Prime.

5. **William Hoffman Prime,** born, N. Y., March 1st 1837; baptized by the Rector of Grace Parish; married at St. Mark's Cathedral, San Antonio, Texas, January 13th 1879, to Anne Rhodes, daughter of the late Edward F. Gilbert, of San Antonio; died at San Antonio June 18th 1881; remains interred 1882 in Greenwood Cemetery, N. Y.; intestate; his widow married Edward II Prime.

Issue.

1. **Charlotte Hoffman Prime,** born, San Antonio, March 23d 1881.

6. **Charlotte Prime,** born, N. Y., November 12th 1838; baptized by the Rector of Grace Parish; married at the residence of her father, 17 West 16th Street, N. Y., December 27th 1858, by the Rector of Grace Parish, to Leonard J., son of the late Leonard J. Wyeth of N. Y.

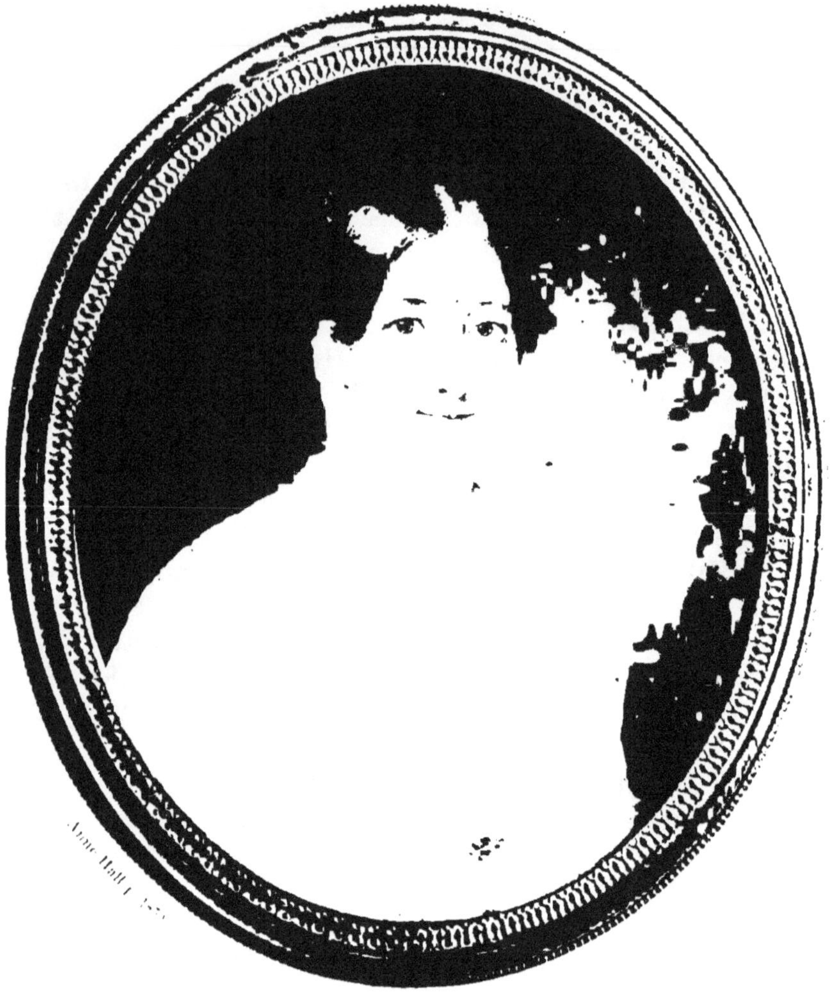

EMILY PRIME,
MRS. WILLIAM SETON.

7. **Emily Mary Prime**, born June 29th 1840; died young.

8. **Mary Catherine Prime,** born, N. Y., June 4th 1841; baptized by the Rector of Grace Parish; married, N. Y., December 16th 1868, by the Rector of Christ Church of Riverdale-on-Hudson, N. Y., to James A., son of James Scrymser of N. Y.

9. **Harriet Prime**, born, August 3d 1843; died young.

10. **Julia Prime**, born, June 6th 1845; died young.

11. **Henry II Prime**, born, N. Y., May 18th 1847; baptized by the Rector of Grace Church.

RUFUS PRIME AND HIS FAMILY.

Born: No. 42 (now 54) Wall Street, N. Y., January 28th 1806; baptized, Grace Church, February 27th 1811.

Died: Huntington, Suffolk co., N. Y., Thursday, October 15th 1885; funeral at Grace Church, N. Y.; interred in Greenwood Cemetery.[1]

Will: N. Y., June 3rd 1879; proved at Riverhead, Suffolk co., N. Y., December 21st 1885; Surrogate's Office, Riverhead, Liber 20, fol. 90.

Married: Philadelphia, October 16th 1828, by Bishop White, to Augusta Temple, daughter of the late William Lambe Palmer, formerly of Ireland, and of Augusta Grenville Temple his wife; she was born, London, England, November 12th 1807; died N. Y., October 9th 1840; in-

---

[1] The shaft in the plot bears upon it the following inscription to his memory:

RUFUS PRIME
Born, New York
XXVIII Jan MDCCCVI
Died, Huntington, N. Y.
XV Oct MDCCCLXXXV.

terred in Greenwood Cemetery;[1] will, N. Y., September 26th 1840, recorded February 5th 1842 in the Office of the Register, N. Y., Liber 423, fol. 199.

Issue.

1. **Frederick Edward Prime,** born in the Casa Altoiti da San Trinita, Florence, Italy, September 24th 1829; baptized Florence, October 12th 1829, by J. L. Parham, Vicar of Holne, co. Devon, England; served in the U. S. army.

2. **Natalie Prime,** born N. Y., March 24th 1831; baptized by the Rector of Grace Parish; died, N. Y., March 19th 1832; interred in Greenwood Cemetery.

3. **Temple Prime,** born, No. 1 Battery Place, N. Y., September 14th, 1832; baptized by the Rector of Grace Parish.

4. **Henry I Prime,** born, N. Y., July 16th 1834; died, N. Y., August 3d 1834; interred in Greenwood Cemetery.

5. **Augusta Prime,** born, N. Y., September 4th 1835; died, N. Y., September 14th 1835; interred in Greenwood Cemetery.

6. **Charles Sandys Prime,** born, No. 1 Battery Place, N. Y., October 16th 1836; baptized by the Rector of Grace Parish: died at Hartford, Conn., December 1st. 1896; funeral at Grace Church, N. Y., on the 4th inst.; interred in Greenwood Cemetery.

---

[1] The shaft in the plot bears upon it the following inscription to her memory:

AUGUSTA TEMPLE
wife of
Rufus Prime
and
daughter of
Wm. L. Palmer
of
Rahan Ireland
Died IX Oct MDCCCXL
ÆT. XXXII.

RUFUS PRIME.

7. **Cornelia III Prime,** born, No. 1 Battery Place, N. Y., December 14th 1838; baptized by the Rector of Grace Parish.

FREDERICK I PRIME AND HIS FAMILY.

Born: 42 (now 54) Wall Street, N. Y., October 30th 1807; baptized, Grace Church, February 27th 1811.

Died: N. Y., July 13th 1887; buried in Beechwood Cemetery, New Rochelle, N. Y.

Will: Surrogate's Office, New York.

Married: 1st, N. Y., April 30th 1829, to Mary Rutherfurd, daughter of Peter A. Jay of N. Y.; she died N. Y., September 9th 1835; interred in the Jay graveyard at Rye, N. Y.

——— 2dly, Providence, R. I., August 15th 1838, to Lydia, daughter of Robert Hare of Philadelphia; she died N. Y., May 24th 1883, in her 65th year; interred in Beechwood Cemetery, New Rochelle; will, July 30th 1859; proved, June 6th 1883; Surrogate's Office N. Y., Liber. 309, fol. 491.

Issue.

1. **Mary Rutherfurd Prime,** born, N. Y., August 24th 1830.

2. **Harriet II Prime,** born, N. Y., September 11th 1832; married, N. Y., at the Church of the Holy Apostles, May 23d 1867, to Thomas P. Gibbons, M. D., of Pennsylvania.

3. **Helen Jay Prime,** born, N. Y., August 22d 1835; married, Pelham, Westchester co., N. Y, October 16th 1856, to Francis T. Garrettson of N. Y.

4. **Emily II Prime,** born, N. Y., August 1st 1840; married, N. Y., at Trinity Chapel, April 23d 1862, to Lewis Livingston, son of Joseph Delafield of N. Y.

5. **Frederick II Prime,** born, Philadelphia, March 1st 1846; married, N. Y., at the Church of the Holy Com-

munion, June 22d 1871, to Laurette de Toussard, daughter of Alfred Coxe, of Philadelphia.

Issue.

1. **Laurette Coxe Prime,** born, May 10th 1872; died at Pelham, August 29th 1873; interred in Beechwood Cemetery at New Rochelle.
2. **Mary Alice Prime,** born, Easton, Pa., June 17th 1874.
3. **Laurette de Toussard Prime,** born, Easton, December 1st 1875.
4. **Frederick III Prime,** born, Philadelphia, September 5th 1879; died, Baltimore, December 17th 1880.
5. **Frederick IV Prime,** born, Baltimore, March 3d 1881.
6. **Alfred Coxe Prime,** born, Philadelphia, March 3d 1883.

MARK I PRIME.

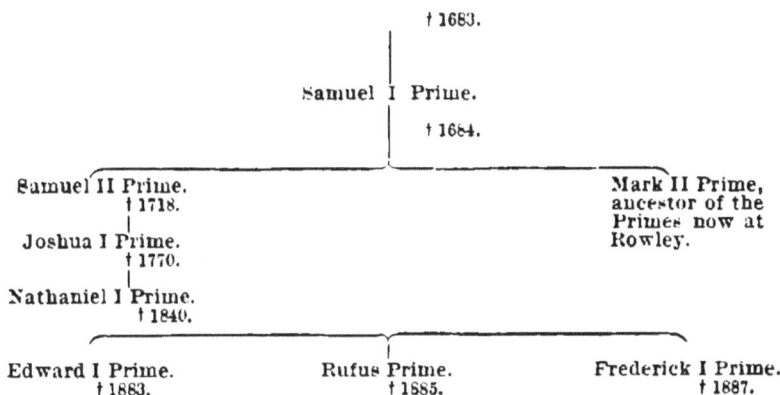

† 1683.

Samuel I Prime.
† 1684.

Samuel II Prime.
† 1718.

Joshua I Prime.
† 1770.

Nathaniel I Prime.
† 1840.

Mark II Prime, ancestor of the Primes now at Rowley.

Edward I Prime.
† 1863.

Rufus Prime.
† 1885.

Frederick I Prime.
† 1887.

AUGUSTA TEMPLE PALMER.
MRS. RUFUS PRIME.

MARK II PRIME, OF ROWLEY, MASS., (SECOND SON OF SAMUEL I PRIME.)

Born: —— baptized, Rowley, March 13th 1680–81.
Died: October 2d 1722 at Rowley; buried there.[1]
Married: February 10th 1702–03, Rowley, Jane, daughter of Thomas Lambert, of Rowley; she was born, Rowley, September 10th, 1685.

Issue.

1. Infant, died April 3rd 1704.
2. **Edna Prime,** born, Rowley, June 15th 1705; married, Rowley, February 16th 1725–26, Eliphalet Payson, of Rowley; she died, Rowley, March 28th 1778.
3. **Jane Prime,** born, Rowley, September 8th 1707; married, November 19th 1730, Nathan, son of Colin Frazer; she married 2dly (subsequently to October 1741), Doctor Eliphalet Kilbourne, of Rowley.
4. **Thomas Prime,** born, Rowley, May 16th 1710; married (published January 24th 1746–47), Abigail Boardman, of Ipswich; he died July — 1796.
5. **Mark Prime,** born, Rowley, February 26th 1712–13; married, Elizabeth ——; had issue a daughter, Olive Prime, baptized, Rowley, February 22d 1735–36. In the Church Records he is styled "Doctor."
6. **Moses Prime,** born, Rowley, August 21st 1715.
7. **Mary Prime,** born, Rowley, August 10th 1719.

---

1 His gravestone bears upon it the following epitaph:

"HERE LIES Y[e] BODY OF
MR MARK PRIME
WHO DIED OCTOBER
Y[e] 7th 1722 IN Y[e]
42 YEAR OF
HIS AGE."

APPENDIX.

Appendix.

Table of Contents of Appendix.

The Settlement at Rowley, Essex co., Mass.

The Revd Ezekiel Rogers was given the living of Rowley,[1] co. York, England by Sir Francis Barrington, co. Essex, Kt.

In December 1638 Mr. Rogers arrived in America with about 20[2] families and they all spent the winter at Salem; April or May 1639 this company, which had increased to 60 families, settled on lands in Essex co., Mass. to which a charter was granted in September 1639, under the name of Rowley.

Soon after the settlement, other families moved into the town, so that before the survey of Rowley, bearing date January 10th 1644, was completed, 16 other families had been added to the original 60, and land was also assigned to them at the time it was distributed.

We find the name of Mark I Prime in the list of the 76 families, but not in that of the 60 families.

These people labored originally in common, and this state of things lasted 5 years, no man owning any land in severalty, until the land on both sides of the brook had been cleared; and they had laid out some streets and roads, several of which received names.

Will of Mark I Prime, and the proving of the same. (PROBATE OFFICE ESSEX CO., MASS., LIBER 4, FOL. 76.)

The last will and testement of Marke Prime of Rowlly being weake in body but ꝑfect in memery doe therefore ordaine this my last will in manner os followeth: I giue my soule to god that gaue it mee and my body to the graue

---

1 Rowley is a parish. 2 or 3 miles from Southcave, in the Wapenstoke of Harthill in the East Riding of Yorkshire, England; in 1831 it had a population of about 500.

2 The names of these 20 families are not known; it is presumed that a list of them was destroyed in 1651, when Mr. Rogers' house was consumed by fire.

with a liuely hope of a joyfull resecrection at the duy of his apear'g as for my outward estate my will is
Imp$^{r.}$ I leaue to my naterall[1] sun Samwell Prime all my housing and lands & medow to be at my suns disposing during his life and to Improue for his own & theire benefit till he dispose of it to those children he now hath or may haue with this wife now liueing and if by the provedence of god he should grow poore and there by be forced to selle any part of lands hee shall sele his own lands and not any of this I now giue,
it is my will and desire that my eldest gron child shall injoy all my lands prouided he make his other brothers & sister equelent to that a part he Inioys in other pay, and also that none of they children shall requir thire leg‾ce of land

goe from vnder their parents

with theire consent according to a rule of the word of god
2 Also it is my will that all my moueable shall be thus deuided that i there be 15 pounds in mony and 5£ in other pay be reaised out of the estat in mouables and be reserued for and equally deuided amongst those children y now are liuing or that be born heare after of this my sun & daughter that are now liuving.

Also it is my will that if moueable estat amount to more than 20£ I leave it to be deuided to the foresaid children at the discresion of my sun and daughter after my desease provided that my daughter Sara be not depriued of Improueing any of the houseuld stufe while she liueth.

Also I apoynt my sun Samuell Prime to be my soale executer of this my last will, And my trusty frends John Haris senr and Samuell Plats senr ouer seers for true purformance of this my last will MARKE PRIME

Witness { JOHN HARRIS
{ SAMUELL PLATTS

---

1 The term "natural" must not be taken to mean "illegitimate"; it was quite common in those days to use this word in describing members of the family. As an example see Historical Collections of the Essex Institute, Vol. XXIII. in which Roger Darby is described in

Probate of the Will.

The Execut^r to this will being deceased before presentation hereof to ye court Letters of Administration to ye estate of Marke Prime are granted unto Sarah Prime ye widow of ye Executor intended & unto Abell Platts, who presented ye Inventorie of ye estate at ye same time and are ordered & enjoyned to attend such orders as this court shall give ab^t settlement of s^d estate Dated At a court of Adjournment held at Ipswich Aprill ye 15 1684 as attest

Jno Appleton Clcr.

An Inuentorie of the estate of Mark Prime deceased taken the 15th of Jany Anno Dom^e 1683 ꝑ subscribers

	£	s.	d.
Imp^r By 7 Acres ½ of Vpland in tillage: & not improued in ye comō feild	18	00	00
It. ꝑ 3 acres of Land in Symonds feild	3	10	00
It. ꝑ marsh at Oyster poynt ꝑ marsh called Carlton's & at Mr Nelsons Isle soe cal^d	20	00	00
It. ꝑ one Oxe Gate in east oxpasture: ½ acr meadow at Shatswell soe cal^d	12	00	00
It. ꝑ Land vpon the Comon 10£ & 1 Freehold 4£	14	00	00
	67	10	00
It. 5 cows 2 young Cattle 2 horses 2 swine	37	10	00
It. ꝑ A Feather bed & furniture peuter & brass earthen: & wooden ware & Iron ware & bookes 1£ & 3 napkins sugar 1 chest & cupboard glasses chaires & table boards silk & thread all amount to	13	11	04
It. ꝑ meat butter meal baggs wheat and Indian corne	7	15	00
It. ꝑ cotton & linnen & woolen cloth & yarne	4	00	00
It. ꝑ Iron & wooden Implements of husbandry & amunition	2	17	00
It. ꝑ mony 6£ 7^s 0^d ꝑ woolen & Linnen cloathes & Apparell 6£	12	7	00
It. ꝑ bills due to ye estate 6£ 17^s 9^d ꝑ other debts 4£ 10^s 0^d all	11	07	09
	156	18	01

---

grants of Letters of Administration in 1671, in two distinct cases, as "natural" brother. Moreover, Samuel's birth is entered on the Records of the Church at Rowley, as the son of Mark and Anne Prime.

The estate Deb

To funerell expences 2£ 15s 0d To other debts 1£ 14s 8d 4 09 08

This Apprizement of the severell ₱ticulars was made ₱ us the day and year above written.

Witness our hands JOHN HARRIS Senr

SAMUEL PLATTS Junier.

Sarah Prime Administratix to the Estate of Marke Prime deceased made oath that the above written is a true Inventory of sd Estate to the best of her Knowledg & if more come to her Knowledg she will give the court an account thereof sworne in court at Ipswich this 15th of Aprill 1684 being held by adjournment.

Attest Bartho Gedney pr ordr

Sarah Prime widow & Abel Plats having power of Administration granted to them on the estate of Samll Prime deceased amounting to 281£ 6s clear of debts this court doth order the distribution of sd estate as followeth viz

Unto the widdow Sarah Prime 80£ 11s unto Samll Prime eldest son of ye deceased 80£ 06s unto Sarah Prime Marke Prime & Añe Prime the rest of the children of the estate to each of them 40£ 3s being 120£ 9s And the whole estate to remain in the possession & to the use of ye widow Sarah Prime for the bringing up the children & paying their portions when they come of age & the houseing and lands stand bound to the court for paymt of ye childrens portions.

And whereas the executor of the will of Mark Prime is deceased & power of administration to sd estate is granted unto ye sd Sarah Prime & Abel Platts this court doth order that they shall Administer upon sd estate according to the tenor of the will of sd Marke Prime that is given in & is on file with ye records of this court.

Agreed Apr 15 1684 in Court.

In re Mark I Prime being a miller.

The herewith affidavit: County Office Salem, Essex co. Mass. 3:71; is among papers in the case of Nelson versus Dummer, March 1657. In an account of Richard Dummer it is mentioned that there was: "paid to Marke Prime for maintaininge the mill damme 10£." "To Goodman Prime for helpe about the millstones 12s." "To Marke Prime for maintaining the mill damme 4 mouth: 54. 0£.—10s—0."

Affidavit.

DEPOSITION OF MARKE PRIME,

"Who saith that the last yeare before Mr. Nelson went away when he and I came to account what the mill got that yeare, the said Mr. Nelson asked me what one halfe of the profits of the mill came unto for that yeare, I answered about sixteen pound he replied his account was there about too since which time I havinge the mill to keep on the same terms from Mr. Richard Dummer to my best understanding I fall not short (for my part of the profits one yeare with another) not above twenty shillings in the yeare and Mr. Dummer had as much for his part of the profits."

Taken upon oath 23d of the 4th month 1656 before me

SAMUELL SYMONDS.

This is a true copie by me

SAMUELL ARCHARD, Marshall.

Settlement of the estate of Samuel I Prime. (PROBATE OFFICE, ESSEX CO., MASS.)

An Inuentorie of ye estate of Samuell Prime deceased ye 18th 1 ^{mo} 1683–04 taken by us whose names are subscribed this 11 April 1684.

	£	s.	d.
Impr^{s} By the dwelling house barne killne & mill & homestead	100	00	00
It. By 7 acres & ½ of vpland: plowing & vnimproued in ye comon feild	18	00	00
It. By 3 acres of land at Symonds brook . . .	3	10	00
It. By marsh at Oysterpoynt by marsh cal^{d} Carltons & at Nelson Isle	20	00	00
It. By marsh cal^{d} Shatswell & marsh cal^{d} highway marsh	6	00	00
It. By 2 ox gates in ye east oxpasture & land in ye commons	30	00	00
177 : 10 : 0			
It. By cattle sheep & swine	34	10	00
It. By wearing clothes & armes	12	17	06
It. By cash in hand & due by Bill from James Bayly all	11	03	00
It. By peuter & tin ware & earthen & wooden ware	03	02	00
It. By Brass & iron ware & vtensells p husbandry books & wood vessells	8	01	00
It. By cloth & Linnen: Yarne: flax: bridle & crooper	9	12	06
It. By a Feather bed & straw bed with Furniture & bedsteads	12	13	00
It. By corne baggs chests boxes bacon saddle & bridle a rug a couerlet & blanket: sives meal & trough a cupboard & Tubs: hops cards salt & sithes &c	16	19	06
It. By a pilliō carpenters tools & a cupboard .	1	04	00
£ s d 110 : 2 : 6			
	287	12	6
It. By Debts due to the estate as now appears .	001	09	0
	289	01	6

It. The estate Deb^r To Funerall charges: & debts which y sent appear 008 15 06½

The severall ℘ticulars according to their value was taken by us the day & year above written witness our hands

NEHEMIAH JEWETT
JOHN HARRIS Senier
SAMUEL PLATTS junier

Sarah Prime Relict widow & administratrix to the estate of Samuell Prime deceased: made oth thet the above written is a true inventory of the estate of Samuell Prime deceased to the best of her knowledg & If she find more she will give acct thereof sworne in court at Ipswich held by adjournment this 15th of Aprill 1684

Attest Barth° Gedney pr ord^r

To the Honered Collolon Giddney Judg of the court of probatts

Your Humble pettioner Samuell Platts would intreat that he may have administration granted to him of the estate of Mark Prime deceased and Samuell Prime the admin deceased and desired

estate into my hands

ake care of her chilldren if she should dye of the sicknes thet then she was in and she did of that sicknes and according to her desire have I done and now the chilldren is near age som of them I would be legally dismissed of it and I am her eldest brother by blood and Samuell Prime her eldest son desires that it may b anted to his uncle Samuell Plats his hand

March the 31: Samuell Prime Essex

ss To the Hon—^ble Barth° Gedney Esqr Judge of probate of wills &c for s^d county March 31th 1696

The Petition of Samuel Plets of Rowley Humbly she to Th ereas Mark Prime dec^d made his will inated his executor to son Samuel Prime who also dec^d the presentation of will to ye county court for propāion & ap where upon ad ācon of the estate of the s^{d} Mark anted unto Sarah P widow of the executor Intended & Plats who w by the s^{d} court to administer a the Tenour of the ll: and whereas Administracon estate of s^{d} Samuell Prime exec^{r} nominated as afores^{d} was also gran to the s^{d} Sarah Prime is Relict together wth the s^{d} Abel Plats hereby they became administrators to both estates and both the administrators being since also dec^{d} & both the said estates being & Remaining in the hands and possession of your petitioner: & your petitioner being desireous to be discharged of the same in such a way as may be safe. Prays that yor Hon^{r} would grant him adm^{con} of the s^{d} estate. In order to a quietus according to Law the eldest son Samuel Prime desireing the same may be confered upon your petitioner

Samuell Platts March 31st 1695/6

administrācon of all & singular the the goodes Chattels Rights & credits of Mark Prime & Sam^{ll} Prime Late of Rowley dec^{d} granted vnto Sam^{ll} Platts Brother in law to Samuell Prime same time giving one thousand pounds bond with Wm Hobson & Joseph Kilborn for sureties.

March 31 1696 Judge Gedney appointed Nehemiah Jewett James Platts Wm Hobson James Baily and Moses Platts all freeholders of Rowley a committee to divide the real estate of Mark Prime and Samuell Prime amongst the widow & children of the said deceased or their legal representatives

These linnes are to signifie that I Mark Prime the son of Samuell Prime deceased and now in my mine oritye do make choise of my uncle James Platts to be my guardian and do pray the honored Judg of probatts that it may be so as wittness my hand this 12 day of Aprill 1697

Marke Prime

Apr 13 1697 James Platts gave bond of four hundred pounds with Sam'l Platts and Benj. Scott for sureties on condition that he be guardian of Mark Prime & of Ann Prime children of Sam^{ll} Prime & Sarah his wife both dec^{d} being minors of one about 13 years ye other 16 years of age.

We whose names are subscribed being commissiōnated by Bartholomew Gedney Esqr judge of probate for the county of Essex to make a division of the houseing & lands of Mark Prime & Samuel Prime late of Rowley decd In pursuance of sd act reference being had to said Mark Primes will who giues his lands paying to the Rest of said Samuels Children the value according to proportions & considering that if sd Samuels eldest son have a double part to the rest in his fathers It will be very ꝑjudiciall & inconvenient to make a distribution of the Lands of said Mark & Samuel the decd into more than two settlements: & therefore judge it best for all the children that said lands belonging to the said Mark & Samuel be setled as hereafter ffollows and that the mony diuidable & moueables in household stuff & other stock be also setled and paid as ffolloweth

Imprs to Samuel Prime sd Samulls eldest son his sd ffathers dwelling house & homestead with a freehold and the mill & Kilne for oatmeal

Item half the tillage land Lying betwixt Mr Northends & Gd man Harris his land in the Comon field being that half next vnto said Harris his land bearing equal length & breadth with the other half

Item three acres of land in the great field caled Simonds field bounded by the brook at one end: on the Southerly side by Edward Hazzens land which is two acres of it: the other acre bounded both sides by Thomas Woods land

Item half the marsh lott called Carletons marsh being that half next John Tods; which his grandfather improved

Item that half of the salt marsh at the oyster poynt next James Dickenson according as was improved by sd Mark

Item half the three acres of meadow at Crane meadow

Item that half of the marsh called Nelson Island marsh being that side lying next to John Pickards marsh with one half of the thatch banck lying at the end of sd marsh wch was the right of Mark Prime aforesd

Item one oxgate & half in the eastend oxepasture wth half that right of land lying in the new oxpasture by ye ky plaine that belongs to sd gate & half

Item half one acre of meadow caled shatswell meadow bounded by Mr Nelsons Southerly side by Mr Thomas Nelsons that was Mr Tods no = west side

Item half the Division of upland Vpon the Comon wch lieth by ye plase caled the streights being that half lying next Thomas Woods land half the length & breadth throughout s^d lott

Item half the Vpland on the comon layd out joyning that Henry Poor bought of Mr Pearson the one half for quantity & quality

Item half the two acre lott on the Town side of the hill called Mr Nelsons hill in the comon field Lying on that side of s^d lott next y^e hill

Item half the planting hill lott lying next ye meadow called Shatswells meadow that half his grandfather improved: with half the vacant land Lying on the no = west of said planting land

Item half the vacant land that was formerly in a pasture: that half lying next Cornet pearsons in Shatswell meadow

To Marke Prime s^d Samuel Prime dec^d his youngest son

Imp^{rs} one half of the three acres of land on the plain in ye comon field lying on that side of s^d lott next Mr Northends land half the length & breadth throughout

Item half the two acre lott on the plain on ye Towne side of the hill called Mr Nelsons hill in the comon field equall breadth & length wth his Bro: Sam^{ls} part

Item three acres of land in the mill field lying on the Westerly side of Jonathan Baylies land

Item half the marsh at the oyster poynt being that side of s^d lott lying next to Jonathan Herrimans marsh

Item half the marsh lot caled Carltons marsh being that side of said lott next Richard Holmes land

Item half the marsh lott at Nelson Island, that side of the lott next to hog Island wch was his fathers half wth one half of the thatch Island in the river at ye end of s^d marsh lott

Item the Division lott in Satchells meadow within Pasture that Mark Prime called two acres

Item half of the vacant Ruff land in said pasture lying next to s^{d} meadow
Item half the planting land at the planting hill lying on that side of s^{d} lott next to the Townes land together with half the Ruff vacant land at the no=west end of sayd planting land
Item all the Division called highway marsh by the way to hog Island
Item one oxgate & half a gate in the east end oxe pasture with the right of land belonging to s^{d} oxgate & half in new oxpasture by the Ky Plaine
Item half the division of wood land by the streights next to the lott which was Charles Brownes
Item half the Division lott vpon the comon next Henry Poors for quantity & quality
Item one freehold or comon right upon the Comons of Rowly
Item one half of the three acres of meadow lying at the meadows caled Crane meadows

To the Daughters viz Sarah & Ann Prime as Followeth
Imp^{rs} It. Sarah & Ann when they come of age or marriage ninety & one pounds each: twenty pounds thereof in money: forty pounds each in quick stock & thirty & six pounds twelve shillings in beding pewter brass & other household stuff
Item whereas there is accounted fourteen pounds five shillings & fourpence left of the widows thirds vnspent wch each hath their proportion in: & s^{d} widow having had one child by her last Husband his proportion with the rest amounts vnto two pounds seven shillings and six pence If it be allowed by ye Hon^{rd} Judge of probate s^{d} Administrator is to pay s^{d} sum vnto Jonathan Bradstreet her youngest child
Item their is allowed besides the lands to Samuell the eldest son a gun a cutlass & half ye Husbandry tooles amounting to fifty shillings
Item to Mark allowed besides the land trooping armes & sadle amounting to three pounds ten shillings

It. Their is allowed to said Administrator Sam[ll] Platts for payments of the s[d] widows debts before sickness & in sickness & funerall charges & payment of taxes & trouble in Administracon the sum of twenty pounds w[ch] we Judge far less than he deserved for his charge and trouble in husbanding the estate above six years

Which settlement if it be allowed by ye Hon[rd] Judge of probate we acct the s[d] children are very well dealt with & according to our Judgment equally distributed amongst them as witness our hands & seals this 8th day of March 1696–7

James Baily [seal]
James Plats [seal]
Moses Plats [seal]
Nehemiah Jewet [seal]

exam[d]
allowed

Know all men by these presents that I James Platts of Rowley guardian for Marke Prime and Ann Prime the son and daughter of Samuell Prime of Rowley deceased do here by these presents acknowledge that I have received of Samuell Platts the full portions of the above said Marke Prime and Ann Prime both in their fathers estate and grandfathers estate and in their mothers thirds according as it was divided and set out to us by men comisioned by the Honoured Judge of probates and I the above said James Platts do hear as guardian to the above said Mark and Ann for ever acquit my Brother Samuell Platts as administrator to the estates of Marke Prime their grandfather and Samuell Prime their father or any other ways in their mothers thirds of any fūther claimes as witness my hand and seall this 14 day of Aprill: 1697 signed sealed and delivered in the presets of us witneses

Nehemiah Jewet James Platts [seal]
Samue Prime

Essex s s James Platts p sonally appeared & acknowledged the above written Instrument to be his act & deed at Ipswich April 14 1697 Before me

Barth[o] Gedney J. P.

Know all men by these presents that I Samuell Prime (the son of Samuell Prime of Rowley deceas[d]) being of twenty one years of age and Sarah Prime the daughter of the above said Samuell deceas[d] aged eighteen years and upward do both of us acknowledg that we have received our full portions of Samuell Platts both in our fathers estate and in our grandfathers estate and also in our mothers thirds according as it was devided and set out to us by men comisioned by the Honoured Judg of probates we for ever quit our uncle Sam[l] Platts as administrators

SAMUEL PRIME [SEAL]
SARAH PRIME [SEAL]

Ack before Bart. Gedney Apr 14 1697

ESSEX CO. PROBATE OFFICE, LIBER 4, FOL. 157.

Captain Moses Bradstreet in his will of August 16th 1690, admitted to probate September 30th 1690, mentioned his wife as follows:

"To my Dear & beloved wife my will is that ye contract before our marriage be fulfilled by my executors that all ye estate reall & personal of hers & her children by her former husband be at her dispose for ye benefit of her & her children and to be paid by her according as ye court settled it: Also that ye fourscore pounds she was to receive by s[d] contract be made up one hundred pounds so much to be made up in household stuffe, as I receved wth her twenty pounds of it in mony & ye rest in cattle & corn such as I received with her Also I give her thirty pounds more one half in money ye other half in corn & cattell to be paid by my executors to ye bringing up of our young child Jonathan."

Settlement of the Estate of Samuel II Prime.

(PROBATE OFFICE, ESSEX CO., MASS.) ESSEX PROBATE, LIBER 12, FOL. 162.

Administration granted to Sarah widow and relict of Saml Prime of Rowley on her husbands estate May 14 1718 at same an inventory of s^{d} estate was presented to the court and an account of said estate was rendered at same time and one of the items in the account was "allowed Towards bringing up 3 children ye youngest being born posthume £45."

ESSEX PROBATE, LIBER 13, FOL. 287.

February 10, 1722–3 Moses Bradstreet was app^{d} guardian of the children of Samuel Prime of Rowley deceased viz:

Samuel Prime, then upwards of 14 years of age
Joshua Prime }
Sarah Prime } " under 14 years of age.

Settlement of Saml Prime's estate, Rowley. ESSEX PROBATE, LIBER 13, FOL. 294.

Samuell Prime of Rowley his estate settled and recorded in Lib 11 folio 160 and then due from the estate £100.. 13.. 7^{d} over and above ye Parsonall estate and whet Debets have been already paid for which the administratrix obtains leave of ye superior court to sell Lands

Lands sold to sundry Persons . . . . £109.. 15.-

To sundry Debts p^{d} as by, receipts here brot. and by acco^{t} on file presented by Robt Rogers Husband to ye said Administratrix shee being deces^{d} 113$^{£}$ 18^{s} 7^{d} itt being 4.. 3.. 7 more than w^{t} y^{e} land sold for . . . . 113.. 18.. 7

The said Robert Rogers duth Ingage to pay to ye estate of ye s^d Deces^d over and above the 4$^£$ 3^s 7^d the sum of Ten pounds and to Deliver all small things that belong to s^d Samuel Prime oat meal mill for the use of the children unto their Guardian and a Gunn appriz^d att 30/

The ten pounds to be paid In Movables that was formerly Samuell Primes as the s^d administratrix received them

Moses Bradstreet as Guardian to s^d Prime's children Receipt

Feb 12th 1722–23 Then Received of Robt Rogers of Rowley the full of all acco^t which was due from him to Sam^{ll} Primes heirs & say rec^d p me

MOSES BRADSTREET Guardian

Settlement of the estate of Joshua Prime. (PROBATE OFFICE, WORCESTER CO., MASS.)

Know all men by these presents that we Bridget Prime of Sutton, widdow, Moody Morss Gent. & Willis Hall, Yeoman all of Sutton in the county of Worcester within His Majesty's Province of the Massachusetts Bay in New England are holden and stand firmly bound and obliged unto John Chandler Esq. Judge of Probate of Wills and granting administrations within the County of Worcester in the full sum of Five hundred Pounds in lawful money of said Province, to be paid unto the said John Chandler, his successors in the said office, or assigns: To the true payment whereof, we do bind ourselves, and each of us, one and each of our heirs, executors and administrators, jointly, and severally, for the whole and in the whole, firmly by these presents.

Sealed with our seals. Dated the twenty-fifth day of July Anno Domini one thousand seven hundred and seventy.

The condition of this present obligation is such that if the above bounden Bridget Prime who is admitted admr.

on ye estate of her late husband Joshua Prime late of said Sutton, Yeoman, des^{d} do make or cause to be made a true and perfect inventory of all and singular the goods, chattels, rights and credits of the said deceased, which have or shall come to the hands, possession or knowledge of her the said Bridget, or into the hands and possession of any other person or persons for her and the same so made, do exhibit or cause to be exhibited into the Registry of the Court of Probate for the said county of Worcester at or before the twenty-fifth day of October next ensuing, and the same goods, chattels, rights and credits and all other the goods, chattels, rights and credits of the said deceased, at the time of his death, which at any time after shall come to the hands and possession of the said Bridget, or into the hands and possession of any other person or persons for her, do well and truly administer according to law: And further do make or cause to be made a just and true accompt of her said administration upon oath, at or before the twenty-fifth day of July which will be in the year of our Lord one thousand seven hundred and seventy-one. And all the rest and residue of the said goods, chattels, rights and credits which shall be found remaining upon the said administratrix accompt (the same being first examined and allowed of by the Judge or Judges for the time being, of Probate of Wills and granting administrations within the County of Worcester aforesaid) and shall deliver and pay unto such person or persons respectively as the said Judge or Judges by his or their decree or sentence pursuant to law shall limit and appoint:

And if it shall hereafter appear that any last will and testament was made by the said deceased, and the executor or executors therein named do exhibit the same into the Court of Probate for the said county of Worcester making request to have it allowed and approved accordingly; if the said Bridget Prime within bounden, being thereunto required, do render and deliver the said Letter of Administration (Approbation of such Testament being first had and made) into the said Court: Then the before written obligation to be void and of none effect, or else to abide and remain in full force and virtue

Sealed and delivered	BRIDGET PRIME [SEAL]
in presence of	MOODY MORSS [SEAL]
CLARK CHANDLER	WILLIS HALL [SEAL]
WILL^{m} CHANDLER	

Province of the Massachusetts Bay, Worcester ss.

To Amos Parsons, Enoch Marble and Stephen Hall all of Sutton, in the county aforesaid. Greeting.

You are hereby appointed and impowered on oath to take an inventory of and (according to your best skill and judgment) truly and justly to apprize (in lawful money of this Province) all the estate whereof Joshua Prime late of Sutton died seized in the aforesaid county: and you are to make return of this Warrant with your doings thereon, unto the Probate Office, in the same county, as soon as conveniently may be.

Given under my hand this twenty-fifth day of July A. D. 1770.

JOHN CHANDLER
Judge Probate.

Worcester ss. August ye 20 1770.

The fore named aprizers appeared and mad oath that they had prizded the forgoing estat according to their best skil and judgment.

Before me

ISAAC BARNARD
Justis of Peace

An inventory of the estate real and personal of which Joshua Prime late of Sutton died seized, as taken by us the subscribers July 26. 1770

The Real Estate	£286.	13.	4
In cash & notes	161.	17.	1
The chattles viz: cattle & swine	26.	4.	0
The husbandry utensels	7.	14.	0
One riding cheir	2.	0.	0
Carried forward	£484.	8.	5

Brought forward	£484.	8.	5
The grain & hay	7.	19.	8
Beds & beding	22.	19.	4
His wareing apparel	10.	6.	10
Brass, iron & wooden wair and all the remainder of ye within door moveables	22.	7.	10
Salt pork	2.	17.	0
Sum total	£550.	19.	1

AMOS PARSONS
ENOCH MARBLE
STEPHEN HALL

Worcester ss. Octo. 7. 1771. Bridget Prime adma on ye estate of her late husband Joshua Prime dec^{d} appeared and made oath that ye aforegoing contains a true & perfect inventory of sd decd. estate so far as has come to her Knowledge & what more shall hereafter appear she will cause to be added.

JOHN CHANDLER
Judge Probate.

Worcester ss. the account of Bridget Prime, admx. on ye estate of Joshua Prime late of Sutton in s^{d} county decd. The said accountant chargeth herself with ye personal estate of said dec^{d} as contained in an inventory thereof exhibited into ye Probate Office for s^{d} county amounting to ye sum of £264. 5. 9

And prays allowance as follows viz:

Pd. Jonathan Dudley		7.	2
Pd. Benj^{a} Mors		6.	10
Pd. Jacob Cummings		6.	0
Pd. Jesse Cummings		8.	8
Pd. Benj^{a} Choate		15.	0
Pd. Elizabeth Plater	5.	16.	9
Pd. Joseph Scott		9.	$5\frac{3}{4}$
Pd. Moody Morss		6.	0
Pd. John Spring	65.	9.	4
Pd. ditto	84.	10.	5
Pd the apprisers		18.	0
Pd Simon Tenny		3.	0
Carried forward	£159.	16.	$7\frac{3}{4}$

Brought forward	£159.	16.	7¾			
Pd Abigail Plumer		4.	10			
Pd Nathl Nighill		8.	4			
Pd David Tenney		3.	0			
Pd William Hale		10.	0			
Pd Jacob Jewett		2.	3½			
Pd Benj^{a} Swinneter		10.	0			
Pd John Nelson		6.	0			
Pd Willis Hall		4.	5			
Pd for adm. & warrant of apprisement		9.	6			
Pd for recording inventory . .		3.	0			
Pd Clark Chandler		18.	5½			
Pd for digging grave		3.	4			
Pd repairs of ye dec^{d} barn . .	2.	3.	0			
Supporting ye apprisers while prising ye estate		6.	0			
Making twenty-four rod fence .		4.	0			
To my trouble administring including a journey to Rowly, a journey to Swansey & 2 journeys to Worcester & 2 to Uxbridge	8.	0.	0			
I pray allowance for ye expense of lying in with a posthumous child	3.	0.	0			
A debt due to Humfry Hoppin I take upon me to pay.		5.	6			
A debt due to Edward Payson I take upon me to pay		1.	10			
A debt due to Joseph Hammond I take upon me to pay . . .	1.	4.	0			
I pray allowance for mourning .	3.	0.	0			
To drawing, allowing & registring this act & a copy . . .		9.	0	179.	15.	1¾
Errors excepted				£84.	10.	7¼

BRIDGET PRIME

Worcester ss. Octo. 7, 1771 Bridget Prime above named appeared & made oath to ye truth of ye above account

JOHN CHANDLER
Judge Probate

Worcester ss. Oct. 14, 1771 Bridget Prime above named presented ye above account for my allowance & having made oath to ye truth thereof and produced vouchers for ye payments therein contained, I allow thereof whereby it appears a ballance remains in her hands of £84. 10. 7¼, one third of said sum belongs to ye said Bridget as her dower being 28. 3. 6¼, ye ballance remaining being £56. 7/ which I order that she pay to ye dec^d^ children, their guardians or legal representatives viz: Samuel, Josiah, Mehetable, Joshua Jewett, Bridgett, Oliver, Nathaniel & Abigail. Saving to ye said Samuel a double share, a single share being £6. 5/2¾

JOHN CHANDLER
Judge Probate.

Worcester ss. To Timothy Sibley, Jacob Commings and Daniel March all of Sutton in the county of Worcester of the Province of the Massachusetts Bay in New England, and sufficient Freeholders,

[SEAL]

Greeting:

Pursuant to the power and authority to me given in and by the laws of said Province, I do hereby authorize and appoint you the above named three persons a committee to apprize all the real estate whereof Joshua Prime late of Sutton in said county, Yeoman, deceased intestate died seiz'd and possess'd (in said Province) in his own proper right in fee simple; each piece and parcel by itself, with their names of distinction, buts and bounds, and number of acres, at the present true value thereof in lawful money, all in words at length.

When you have perfected your inventory, you are to set off to Bridget Prime (the said deceased's widow) one full third part of the said estate (so as may be convenient for her) for her dower or thirds during her natural life; and what you so sett off you are to describe by plain and lasting meets and bounds, that so confusion may be prevented upon the reversion of the dower. The remainder you are to distribute to and among the children of the said deceased, or so many of them as the same will conveniently accommodate, without prejudice to or spoiling the whole, preference being had to the sons. And in all deal impartially as you are sworn, to the eldest son a double share.

Moreover if any of the children of the said deceased have received anything of him in his lifetime in advance towards their portions, you are to signify the same to me and how much each one has had.

When you go about your work, let all parties concerned have notice; and if any dispute arise about the quantity, of any parcel of land, you may procure an artist for the survey thereof; and if all said parties are satisfied with your proceedings let them signify the same by countersigning.

Finally, seal up this commission with your doings thereon, and return the same with all convenient speed, into the Register's Office of Probate by some or one of yourselves.

Given under my hand and seal of office this seventh day of October Anno Domini one thousand and seven hundred and seventy-one, and in the eleventh year of his Majesty's Reign.

John Chandler
Judge Probate

Worcester ss. Oct^{br} 21, 1771. The within named three persons (viz) Jacob Coming, Daniel March, Timothy Sibley appeard and maid solom oath that in apprizeng and deviding the reail estate of Joshua Prim late of Sutton dec^{d} yeoman thay acted imparicaly acording to theair beste skil and judgemonte.

Befour me

Isaac Barnard
Justes a peace.

Pursuant to a commission to us directed from the Hon^{l} John Chandler Esq. Judge of Probate &c for the county of Worster for apprising & dividing the real estate of Joshua Prime late of Sutton dec^{t} Said estat lyeth in Sutton in s^{d} county.

To one hundred thirteen acres of land and buildings apprized at	£251. 13. 10
Set off to Bridget Prime (said deceased's widow) thirty five acres and one hundred & thirteen pole and buildings apprized at	£83. 16. 10

Said land is buted & bounded as followeth (viz): the first piece containing one acre & eleven pole with the easterly part of the dwelling house, the easterly part of the barn & Black smith shop thereon, bounded as followeth, beginning at a stake and stones in the yard before the doors & two rod westerly from a mile stone, then North sixteen degrees West through the houss eight rod to a stake & stones, then West sixteen deg^{s} South two rod & ½ to a stake & stones by the barn yard: then North 26 deg^{s} West through the medle of the barn 6 rod to a stake & stones; then westerly about two rod to rod to the road; then northerly about 10 rod by the s^{d} road to a heep of stones at Willis Hall's land; then easterly by s^{d} Hall's land thirteen rod to a heep of stones; then South 3° East 11 rod & ½ to a stake & stones; then South 25° east 6 rod to a stake & stones at the country road; then westerly by said road 7 rod & ½ to the bounds first mentioned.

The second piece containing 25 acres & 62 pole lying on the south side the contry road and the easterly side of the south lot. Beginning at a heep of stones at Willis Hall's land; then southerly bounding on said Hall's part & part on Stephen Hall's land 150 rod to a stake & stones; then westerly by Edmund Peters land 27 rod to a stake and heep of stones; then north 33° West 152 rod by land set off to the heirs of s^{d} dec^{t} to a stake & stones at s^{d} country road; then easterly by s^{d} road about 28 rod to the bounds first mentioned, giveing her full liberty to pass & repass through other land as necessity shall require whear it will dow least damige.

The third piece containing 9 acres & 40 pole being part of the parster called the How paster. Beginning at a stake & stones the north side of the country road; then West 43° South by s^{d} road 27 rod to a stone at Jacob Commings land; then North 32° West bounding on s^{d} Commings 57 rod to a heep of stones; then East 36° North by land of s^{d} heirs 25 rod to a heep of stone; then southerly by land of s^{d} Commings to the bounds first mentioned reserving liberty of passing & repassing to the other part of s^{d} paster.

The above s^{d} three pieces together with the building we apprize to be one full third part of s^{d} dect^{s}. real estate.

Set off to Samuel Prime the oldest son of s^{d} dec^{t}. 18 acres of land, it being the remaining part of the above said How paster apprized at £37. 6. 0 and is bounded as followeth (viz) beginning a heep of stones, the southwest corner of s^{d} land; then North 32° West by land of s^{d} Commings 36 rod to a heep of stones at Malicha Marble's land a corner; then North 36° East, part by s^{d} Malicha and part by Enoch Marble's land 86 rod & a half to stones by a stump; then South 32° East 31 rod & a half bounding part on John Nelson & part on s^{d} Commings to a stake & stones; then South 28° West on s^{d} Commings 22 rod to a stake & stones; then South 33° West on s^{d} Commings 40 rod to a stake & stones; then Southeasterly on s^{d} Commings 8 rod to a heep of stones; then West 36° South bounding on land set of to the widow 25 rod to the bounds first mentioned with liberty to pass & repass thro that part of ye widows thirds to the country road. It being the full of s^{d} Samuel two shears in said real estate of the above s^{d} dec^{t}.

Set off to Josiah Prime second son of s^{d} Joshua Prime dec^{t}. ten acres and 76 pole with the remaining part of the buildings (viz) the west end of the house & barn apprized at £18. 13. 0.

The first piece containing 40 pole is bounded as followeth

(viz) begonning at a stake & stones before the door 2 rod from the mile stone, then North 16° West throug the house 8 rod to stake & stones, then West 16° South 2 rod & a half to a stake & stones by the barn yard, then North 26° West through the barn 6 rod to a stake & stones; then westerly 2 rod to the town road; then South 30° East on s^d road 14 rod to a stake & stones at the country road; then easterly on s^d country road to the bounds first mentioned. And also another piece containing ten acres & 36 pole lying in the south lot and is bounded as followeth (viz) beginning at a stake & stones the north west corner of the widow's thirds: then South 33° East bounding on s^d widows thirds 152 rod to a stake & stones at s^d Potters land; then West 26° South 11 rod on s^d Potters to a stake & stones; then northerly 152 rod to a stake & stones at the above said country road; then easterly bounding on said road 11 rod to the bounds first mentioned, giveing him the privelidge of passing & re-passing thro any of the other lots to any part of the above last decribed lot where it shall be left to the damage of any of s^d lots as necessity shall reqire him, also resarveing liberty to the widow to pass & repass thro s^d lot as necessity shall require. The above s^d lands & building being one full sheir in s^d real estate of the above s^d dec^t.

Set off to Joshua Jewett Prime third son of s^d Joshua Prime dec^t 7 acres & 96 pole of land apprized at £18. 13. 0 and is butted & bounded as followeth (viz) Begining at a stake & stones the north west corner of the above s^d Josiah's lot: then southerly bounding on s^d Josiah's lot 152 rod to a stake & stones at Potter's land; then West 26° South on s^d Potter's land 9 rod to a stake & stones; then northerly 153 rod to a stake & stones at s^d country road; then easterly bounding on s^d road 7 rod to the bounds first mentioned. Giveing him the privelidge of passing & repassing thro any of the other lots as necessity shall require — & lest to the damige of said lots. Also reserveing liberty for any of the other lots passing & repassing through his the said Joshua's lot as necessity shall require & last to the damige. The within discribed land of 7 acres & 96 pole is one full share of s^{d} real estate of the above s^{d} dec^{t}..

Set off to Oliver Prime fourth son of s^{d} Joshua Prime dec^{t}. 7 acres 104 pole of land apprized at £18. 13. 0 and is butted & bounded as followeth (viz) begining at a stake & stones at the country road; then southerly bounded on the above s^{d} Joshua Jewett's lot 153 rod to a stake & stones at the before s^{d} Potter's land; then westerly on s^{d} Potter's land 8 rod & a half to a stake & stones: then northerly 155 rod to an elm tree marked at s^{d} road; then easterly by s^{d} road 8 rod to the bounds first mentioned, giveing him the privelidge to pass & repass thro any of the other lotts as necessity shall require whear it will dow least damig; also reserveing liberty for any of the other lotts to pass & repass thro s^{d} Oliver's lot as necessity shall require whear it will do least damige. The above described 7 acres & 109 pole being one full shair of s^{d} real estate of the above s^{d} dec^{t}.

Set off to Nathaniel Prime fifth son of Joshua Prime dec^{t} 7 acres & 10 pole of land apprized at £18. 13. 0 and is butted & bounded as followeth (viz) begining at an elm tree marked at s^{d} country road; then southerly bound on the above s^{d} Oliver's lot 155 rod to a stake and stones at s^{d} Potter's land: then westerly 7 rod & ½ to a stake & stones: then northerly 158 rod to a stake & stones a s^{d} road; then easterly on s^{d} road 7 rod to the bounds first mentioned. Resarving liberty for any of the other lots to pass & repass thro s^{d} Nathaniel's lot as necessity shall require. The above described 7 acres & 10 pole being the one whole shair of the s^{d} real estate of s^{d} dec^{t}.

Set off to Mehetabel Prime eldest daughter of s^{d} Joshua Prime dec^{t}, six acres & 35 pole of land apprized at £18. 13. 0 and is butted & bounded as followeth (viz) beginiug at a stake and stones at s^{d} country road; then runing southerly bounding on the above s^{d} Nathaniel's lot 158 rod to a stake & stones at s^{d} Potter's land; then westerly 7 rod bounding on s^{d} Potter's land to a stake and stones; then northerly 158 rod to a stake & stones at s^{d} road; then easterly bounding on sd road 6 rod & 10 links to the bounds first mentioned. Giveing to her the sd Mehetabel the previledge to pass & repass thro any of the other lots as necessity shall require; also reserveing liberty for the owner or owners of any of the other lots to pass & repass thro sd lot as necessity shall require. The above decribed 6 acres & 35 poles being one full shair of the sd real estate of sd decd.

Set off to Bridget Prime, second daughter of sd Joshua Prime decsd 7 acres & 50 pole of land apprized at £18. 13. 0 and is butted & bounded as followeth (viz) begining at a stake and stones at the country road; then southerly bounding on Mehetabel lot 158 rod to a stake & stones at sd Potter's land: then westerly bounding on sd Potter's land 8 rod to a stake & stones, it being a corner of Joseph Sherburn Esqr land; then northerly bounding on sd Sherburns land 156 rod to a heep of stones at sd road; then easterly bounding on sd road 8 rod to the bounds first mentioned. Giveing her, the said Bridget, liberty to pass & repass thro any of the other lotts as necessity shall require. The above described 7 acres & 50 poles being the full of one shair in the sd real estate of sd decd.

Set off to Abigail Prime, third daughter of sd Joshua Prime dect 12 acres & a half of land apprized at £18. 13. 0 and is butted & bounded as followeth (viz) Begining at a heep of stones, it being the southeasterly corner on the north side of sd country road; then westerly bounding on sd road 33 rod to a stake & stones at Jacob Commings land; then northerly about 2 rod on sd Commings to a heep of stones; then West 13° North 19 rod bounding on sd Commings to corconut tree markd; then West 36° North 7 rod & ¾ on sd Comings to a stake & stones; then West 1 rod & a half to a stake & stones; then North 7° West bounding on sd Commings 16 rod & a half to a stake & stones; then North 12° West on sd Comming 19 rod & three quarters to a stake & stones at John Nelson's land; then easterly by sd Nelson land aboot 33 rod to a heep of stones at the town road; then southeasterly and southerly bounding on sd town road to the bounds first mentioned. The above described 12 acres & a half is one full shair of the said real estate of the above s[d] dec[t].

To the above settlement all parties consarned have agreed

Sutton Oct[r] 19, 1771.

JACOB COMMINGS
DANIEL MARCH
TIMOTHY SIBLEY } Com[tee]

BRIDGET PRIME
WILLIAM TODD Guardian for Sam[l] Prime

BRIDGET PRIME as guardian for
JOSIAH PRIME
JOSHUA JEWETT PRIME
OLIVER PRIME
NATHANIEL PRIME
MEHETABEL PRIME
BRIDGET PRIME
ABIGAIL PRIME

Com[s] charge	Timothy Sibley 4 days	£1. 0. 0
	Jacob Comings 4 days & pay to Justice	14.
	Daniel March 4 days & going to Worcester	14.
		2. 8. 0

Worcester ss. To all people to whom these presents shall come. John Chandler Esq. Judge of ye Probate of Wills &c in ye county of Worcester within ye Province of ye Massachusetts Bay in New England sends greeting.

Know ye that pursuant to ye laws of ye said Province relative to the settlement of ye estates of Intestates & the disrection, power & authority to me therein given, I do hereby accept of ye doings of ye comittee by me appointed for ye apprising & dividing ye real estate of Joshua Prime late of Sutton in s[d] county, yeoman, dec[d] hereto annexed & for setting of unto Bridget Prime, ye said dec[d] widdow her dower therein & which at her Death must suffer a division among ye proven heirs that may then be agreeable to law.

I do also assign unto Samuel Prime, Josiah Prime, Joshua Jewett Prime, Oliver Prime, Nathaniel Prime, Mehetable

Prime, Bridget Prime & Abigail Prime children of said deceased & to their respective heirs & assigns ye land to them respectively held pr s[d] return to be by them severally held & enjoyed and order ye same to be recorded, and whereas the charge of said division amounts to ye sum of four pounds six shillings & sixpence. I order that each heir pay his respective proportion according to their interest therein.

In testimony whereof I have hereto set my hand & seal at ye Court of Probate for s[d] county this eighth day of June Anno Dom. 1772 & in ye twelfth year of his Majesty's reign

JOHN CHANDLER

Cost Warrant of assignment		2.	6
Ye comittee & their oath	2.	8.	0
Acceptance		3.	
Record & copy		16.	0
Exed		1.	
Suggesting of Comittee		10.	
1 day of ye adv to procure a Com to dive of estate.		6.	
	£4.	6.	6

Residences of Nathaniel I Prime in New York.

April 1792, 16 Duke Street.

October 1792, May 1793, } 13 Maiden Lane.

June, August 1793, 1 Broadway (a boarding-house).

1796-1797, 1 Broadway (a boarding-house).

1797-1798, 26 Pine Street (the residence of his father-in-law, Comfort Sands).

1799, 79 Greenwich Street.

1800, 146 Washington Street.

1801-1810, 42 (now 54) Wall Street.

1810-1831, 1 Broadway (his property).

1831-1840, Hell Gate, 86th Street, N. Y.

Residences of Rufus Prime.

1829-1840, 1 Battery Place, N. Y.
1840-1843, Hell Gate, 86th Street, N. Y.
1843-1846, in Europe.
1846-1854, Hell Gate, 86th Street, N. Y.
1854-1885, 113 (now 147) West 14th Street, N. Y.
1855-1885, Huntington, Suffolk co., N. Y.

Family Vault at East Chester, Westchester co., N. Y.

The vault is outside of St. Paul's Church, near the south-east wall.

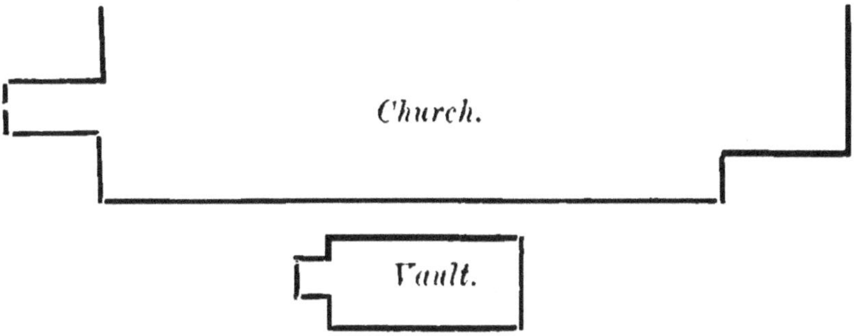

Deeded October 25th 1843,[1] to Cornelia, widow of Nathaniel I Prime.

PORTRAITS, etc., OF MEMBERS OF THE FAMILY.

Nathaniel I Prime.

		Owner.
1.	Miniature[2]	E. L. Coster.
	Copy of same on porcelain . .	Cornelia Prime.

[1] The deed was formerly in the possession of Frederick I Prime.
[2] See accompanying reproduction.

	Owner.
2. Oil painting by Trumbull, taken in 1805	Cornelia Prime Lowell.
Copy of same	Temple Prime.
3. Bust in marble by Frazee	Frederick Prime.

Cornelia Sands, wife of Nathaniel I Prime.

	Owner.
1. Miniature [1]	E. L. Coster.
Copy of same on porcelain	Cornelia Prime.
2. Oil painting by Trumbull, taken in 1805	Cornelia Prime Lowell.
Copy of same	Temple Prime.
3. Represented with her granddaughter Emily Ray; miniature by Miss Anne Hall, taken in 1826	Mrs. Baylies.
4. Miniature by Miss Anne Hall, taken in 1845 [1]	

Cornelia I Prime, Mrs. Ray.

	Owner.
1. Miniature taken by Collas in 1819	
2. Miniature	Mrs. Baylies.

Edward I Prime.

	Owner.
1. Oil painting by R. Peale, taken in 1822	Edward Prime.

---

[1] See accompanying reproduction.

Anne Bard, first wife of Edward I Prime.

	Owner.
1. Miniature by Miss Anne Hall .	Edward Prime.
2. Represented with her children, Cornelia, Nathaniel and William Bard, miniature by Miss Anne Hall	Edward Prime.

Charlotte W. Hoffman, second wife of Edward I Prime.

	Owner.
1. Miniature by Miss Anne Hall, taken in 1836	

Emily I Prime, Mrs. Seton.

	Owner.
1. Miniature by Collas, taken in 1821	Henry Seton.
2. Miniature by Millet, taken in 1827	Henry Seton.
3. Miniature by Miss Anne Hall, taken in 1850[1]	Robert Seton.

Rufus Prime.

	Owner.
1. Miniature by Millet, taken in 1828[1]	Temple Prime.
Copy of same on porcelain . .	Cornelia Prime.
2. Crayon taken in 1829	Cornelia Prime.
3. Oil painting by D. Huntington, taken in 1877	Cornelia Prime.
Copy of same	New York Chamber of Commerce.

[1] See accompanying reproduction.

Augusta Temple Palmer, wife of Rufus Prime.

	Owner.
1. Miniature by Isabey, taken in Paris in 1828[1]	Cornelia Prime.
Copy of same on porcelain . . .	Cornelia Prime.
2. Miniature taken by Miss Anne Hall in 1840	Frederick T. Palmer.
Copy of same on porcelain . . .	Cornelia Prime.

Frederick Edward Prime.

	Owner.
1. Miniature by Aimée Thibault, taken in 1833	Cornelia Prime.
2. Colored drawing, taken in Paris in 1843, by Numa Blanc . . .	Cornelia Prime.

Temple Prime.

	Owner.
1. Miniature, taken in London in 1838	Cornelia Prime.
2. Colored drawing, taken in New York in 1840	Cornelia Prime.
3. Colored drawing, taken in Paris in 1843, by Numa Blanc . . .	Cornelia Prime.
4. Oil painting, cabinet size, taken in Versailles in 1854, by Grolig	F. T. Palmer.

Charles Sandys Prime.

	Owner.
1. Colored drawing, taken in Paris in 1843, by Numa Blanc . . .	Cornelia Prime.

---

[1] See accompanying reproduction.

Cornelia III Prime.

Owner.

1. Colored drawing, taken in Paris in 1843, by Numa Blanc . . . Cornelia Prime.

Frederick I Prime.

Owner.

1. Miniature, taken by Inman in 1829 . . . . Mary R. Prime.
2. Oil Painting, taken by Weir in 1830 . . . . Mary R. Prime.
3. Oil painting, taken by D. Huntington in 1872 . . . . Mary R. Prime.

Mary Rutherfurd Jay, first wife of Frederick I Prime.

Owner.

1. Miniature, taken in childhood with her mother . . . .
2. Oil painting, taken by Ingham in 1825 . . . . Mrs. Garrettson.
3. Oil painting, taken by Trumbull in 1829 . . . . Mary R. Prime.
4. Represented with her daughter Harriet, miniature, taken in 1834 by Miss Anne Hall . . . Mrs. Gibbons.

Lydia Hare, second wife of Frederick I Prime.

Owner.

1. Miniature, taken by Miss Anne Hall in 1840 . . . . Mrs. Delafield.

Mary Rutherfurd Prime.

	Owner.
1. Represented with her sister Harriet, pastel, taken in Geneva in 1848	
2. Oil painting, taken in Rome in 1868	

Helen Jay Prime, Mrs. Garrettson.

	Owner.
1. Crayon, taken in 1858, by Mrs. Childs	

Emily II Prime, Mrs. Delafield.

	Owner.
1. Miniature, taken by Miss Anne Hall in 1845	Mrs. Delafield.
2. Represented with her brother, pastel, taken in Geneva in 1848 .	
3. Oil painting, cabinet size, taken by D. Huntington in 1863 . .	

Frederick II Prime.

	Owner.
1. Oil painting, cabinet size, taken in Dresden in 1867	

Matilda Prime, Mrs. Coster.

	Owner.
1. Miniature	E. L. Coster.

Laura Prime, Mrs. Jay.

	Owner.
1. Represented with her daughter Laura, miniature, taken in 1833 by Miss Anne Hall	Mrs. Wurts.
2. Oil painting by D. Huntington .	

Obituary Notice of Daniel N. Prime, of Rowley, a descendant of Mark II Prime. (ESSEX CO. MERCURY, DECEMBER 21st, 1881.)

The death of Capt. Daniel N. Prime, which occurred during the last week, has been noticed in the daily papers, but is deserving of more than a passing mention on account of his advanced age and the prominent position which he occupied in the town during a long and useful life, managing at one time the business of a country store, tannery, shoe manufactory, and a small farm. When the Eastern Railroad was opened through the town, he was among the few who became interested in the enterprise, purchasing at that time the land through which the road to the station was opened, and also a tract of swamp land lying along the borders of the marsh, containing some thirty or forty acres, all of which he reclaimed and converted into valuable mowing. He was the first station-master upon the railroad in this town, and established a line of freight wagons between Rowley and Georgetown, which was continued until the opening of the railroad through the latter town. In his earlier days he was frequently chosen to town offices, and twice filled the position of Representative to the General Court.

The deceased has from time to time exhibited considerable literary talent, several of his productions in poetry as well as prose having been printed and enjoyed by those who knew him best. He was the author of an ode sung at the centennial celebration of the settlement of the town in 1839, and in those earlier days wrote several poems upon local subjects which interested and amused his townsmen. During his later years his mind has been more particularly exercised upon religious topics and made familiar with the Bible and theological works. He was an earnest advocate of the doctrine of universal salvation, and those who differed from him in conviction gave him credit for honesty, sincerity, and a kindly disposition toward all. For several years he has been deprived of sight, and, by this misfortune, of his favorite pastime of reading and writing.

The physicians in attendance could discover no appearance of disease of any kind; death seemed the result of natural decay — reaching the end "like a shock of corn fully ripe." The funeral services were conducted by the Rev. Mr. Closson of Essex, on Friday afternoon, in the chapel of the Universalist parish. The house was crowded with neighbors and friends. Many were noticed from the adjoining towns, drawn by the influence of old memories and associations. The officiating clergyman, who formerly supplied the desk in which he stood, and enjoyed the acquaintance of the deceased, spoke at length of his pure and exemplary life; and when he declared his belief that no person could point the finger at the casket and say that its inmate had ever done his neighbor wrong, the assertion met with a response in every bosom, and brought moisture to many eyes.

The partnership title of "D. N. Prime & Sons" is still retained by the sons, both in trade and manufacture, and an older or more honorable name cannot be found in commercial circles.

SOME ACCOUNT OF THE PLATTS FAMILY, OF ROWLEY.

SAMUEL I PLATTS.

Died: prior to 1690.

Married: 1st, Sarah; she died, Rowley, April 10th 1681.

——— 2ndly, Rowley, December 19th 1682, Philippa Felt, of Salem (probably a widow); she married again, April 9th 1690, at Rowley, Thomas Nelson, of Rowley; she died, September 29th 1709.

Issue.

1. **Samuel II Platts,** born (probably in England), 1648; died, Rowley, March 24th 1726, buried there;[1] married, Rowley, April 4th 1678, Mary, daughter of William Law; she died, Rowley, June 2nd 1726, buried there;[2] left no issue male.

2. **Abel I Platts,** of whom later.

3. **Elizabeth Platts,** married, Rowley, November 22nd 1681, Samuel Brocklebank, of Rowley.

4. **Sarah Platts,** born, Rowley, October 16th 1654; married, Rowley, January 1st 1673, Samuel I Prime; she married, 2ndly, Moses Bradstreet, of Ipswich, Mass.; she died prior to 1696.

---

(1) His gravestone bears the following epitaph:
"HERE LIES Ye
BODY OF MR
SAMUEL PLATS
WHO DIED
MARCH Ye 24
1726 IN Ye
78 YEAR OF
HIS AGE"

(2) Her gravestone bears the following epitaph:
"HERE LIES THE
BODY OF MRs MARY
PLATS Ye WIFE OF
MR SAMUEL PLATS
WHO DIED JUNE
Ye 2ND 1726 IN Ye
70th YEAR OF HER
AGE"

5. **James Platts,** born, Rowley, June 11th 1661; married, Rowley, September 10th 1691, Lydia, daughter of Thomas Hale, of Newbury, Mass; he died, Rowley, August 26th 1742; left issue male.

6. **Mary Platts,** baptized, Rowley, June 29th 1684.

Account of Samuel I Platts.

Came to Rowley, with first wife and three children, *circa* 1654.

Representative in 1681.

Abel I Platts.

Born: ——, probably in England.

Died: in Canada in 1690.

Married: Rowley, May 8th 1672, Lydia, daughter of James Bailey, of Rowley; she was born, Rowley, November, 1642; she married, 2ndly, Captain Daniel Wicom, of Rowley; she died, Rowley, November 24th 1722; buried there.[1]

Issue.

1. **Moses I Platts,** of whom later.

2. **Abel II Platts,** baptized, Rowley, June 13th 1675; died prior to 1694.

---

(1) Her tombstone bears the following epitaph:

HERE LIES
THE BODY OF
MRS LIDIEA
WICOM THE
WIFE OF CAPT
DANIEL WICOM
WHO DIED Ye
24 OF NOUEM
BER 1722
AGED 80 YEARS

3. **Hannah Platts,** baptized, Rowley, February 23rd 1678–79; married, August 26th 1701, Samuel Lancaster; he died at Rowley in 1710; she married 2ndly, in 1713, Thomas Hammond, of Ipswich.

4. **Samuel III Platts,** born, Rowley, February 5th 1681–82; died prior to 1694.

Account of Abel I Platts.

Ensign in the Rowley Company in the Canada Expedition; died in "ye Canada Voyage."

Inventory of estate July 28th 1691; estate divided March 26th 1694; widow and children, Moses and Hannah, mentioned. (Probate Office, Essex co., Mass., Liber 3, fol. 152.)

MOSES I PLATTS.

Born: Rowley, February 4th 1672–73.

Died: Rowley, March 30th 1739.

Will: March 28th 1739; proved April 23rd 1739. (Probate Office, Essex county, Mass., Liber 24, fol. 24.)

Married: Rowley, November 22nd 1693, Hannah, daughter of Jonathan Platts, of Rowley, by Elizabeth Johnson, his wife; she was baptized at Rowley, April 15th 1676; she died, Rowley, March 31st 1755.

Issue.

1. **Abel III Platts,** baptized, Rowley, August 26th 1694; died young.

2. **Lydia Platts,** born March 20th 1695–96; married November 22nd 1716, Moses Pickard of Rowley; she died April 1st 1774.

3. **Elizabeth Platts,** born February 8th 1698–99.

4. An infant, died July 16th 1701, unbaptized.

5. **Hannah Platts**, baptized November 8th 1702; died December 10th 1702.

6. **Abel IV Platts**, born February 6th 1703–04; married April 21st 1725, Mary Varnum.

7. **Moses II Platts**, born April 9th 1707; married December 2nd 1731, in Gloucester, Mass., Ruth Williams, of that place; he died in 1745, leaving issue male; his widow had subsequently two husbands, Jabez Blackledge, and Samuel Clark, of Gloucester.

8. **Hannah Platts**, born March 27th 1710; married April 4th 1732, John Carlton, of Bradford, Mass.

9. **Mehetable Platts**, born, Rowley, November 11th 1712; married, Rowley, January 1st 1733–34, Joshua Prime; she died, Rowley, October 17th 1751.

10. **Nathan Platts**, born July 23rd 1715; married March 4th 1739–40, Elizabeth, daughter of Edward Saunders; they were dismissed from the Church at Rowley, November 7th 1750, to that of Lunenburg.

11. **Johnathan Platts**, born November 10th 1719; died June 4th 1736.

SAMUEL PLATTS.

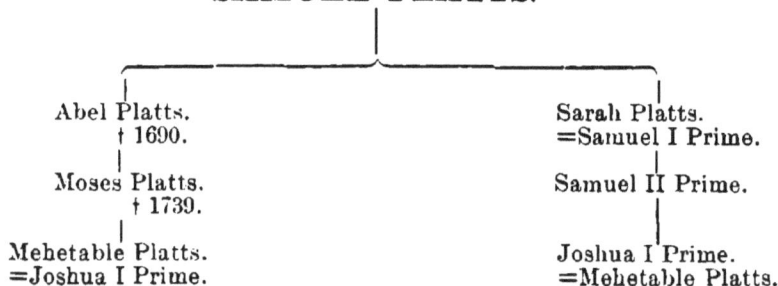

Abel Platts. † 1690.	Sarah Platts. =Samuel I Prime.
Moses Platts. † 1739.	Samuel II Prime.
Mehetable Platts. =Joshua I Prime.	Joshua I Prime. =Mehetable Platts.

SOME ACCOUNT OF THE JEWETT FAMILY, OF ROWLEY.

EDWARD JEWETT,

(OF BRADFORD, WEST RIDING OF CO. YORK, ENGLAND, CLOTHIER.[1])

Married: Bradford, England, October 1st 1604, Mary, daughter of William Taylor.

Will: February 2d 1614–15; proved by his widow, executrix, July 12th 1616. (Officer of the Archdiocese of York, England.)[2]

Issue.

1. **William Jewett,** baptized, Bradford, England, September 15th 1605.
2. **Maximillian Jewett,** baptized, Bradford, England, October 4th 1607; settled at Rowley, Mass.; died October 19th 1684; left issue male.
3. **Joseph I Jewett,** of whom later.
4. **Sarah Jewett,** baptized, Bradford, England, August 31st 1613.

JOSEPH I JEWETT.

Born: ——; baptized, Bradford, England, December 31st 1609.

Died: ——; buried, Rowley, Mass., February 26th 1660–61.

Will: February 15th 1660–61; proved March 26th 1661. (Probate Office, Essex co., Mass.)[3]

---

[1] By clothier, is to be understood, a maker of cloth, a manufacturer; in that sense only was the term used in England in those times.

[2] See page 77. [3] See page 78.

Married: 1st, Bradford, England, October 1st **1634**, Mary Mallinson.

——— 2dly, Boston, Mass., May 13th 1653, Anne, widow of Bozoan Allen, of Boston; she was buried at Rowley, February 18th 1660–61; her will, dated February 5th 1660–61, was proved May 2d 1661. (Essex Probate.)

Issue.

1. **Jeremiah Jewett,** born *circa* 1637; married, Rowley, May 1st 1661, Sarah, daughter of Thomas Dickinson, of Rowley; he died, Rowley, May 20th 1714; buried there;[1] left issue male.

2. **Sarah Jewett,** married, Rowley, June 24th 1657, Captain Philip Nelson, of Rowley; she was buried at Rowley, February 17th 1665–66.

3. **Hannah Jewett,** born, Rowley, June 15th **1641**; married 1st, John Carlton, 2dly, Christopher Babbage, of Salem, Mass.

4. **Nehemiah Jewett,** born, Rowley, April 6th 1643; married in Lynn, Mass., October 19th 1668, Exercise, daughter of John Pierce, of that place; he died at Rowley, January 1st 1719–20, and was buried there;[2] left issue male.

---

[1] His tombstone bears upon it the following epitaph:

HERE LYS Ye BODY OF
IEREMIAH IEWET
WHO DIED MAY
Ye 20 1714
AGED 77

[2] His tombstone bears upon it the following epitaph:

HERE LYES WHAT
WAS MORTAL
OF Ye WORTHY
NEHEMIAH JEWET,
VESQUIER∧
WHO DIDE IANUARY
Ye 1st 1719–20 AGED
77·YEARS · LACKING
3 MONTHES

5. **Faith Jewett,** died in infancy.

6. **Patience Jewett,** twin of Faith, born, Rowley, May 5th, 1645; married in Lynn, May 29th, 1666, Shubeal Walker, of Bradford, Mass.

7. **Mary Jewett,** born, Rowley, April 4th 1654; died in infancy.

8. **Joseph II Jewett,** of whom later.

9. **Faith Jewett,** married in Ipswich, May 20th 1678, John Pingry, of that place.

Account of Joseph I Jewett.

It is presumed that he and his brother Maximilian came to Rowley with the Rev. Ezekiel Rogers, in 1639.

May 22d 1639, freeman; in 1643 he had assigned to him at Rowley a two acre lot on Bradford Street; representative from 1651–54, and again in 1660.

JOSEPH II JEWETT.

Born: April 1st 1656.

Died: October 30th 1694.

Married: January 16th 1680–81, Ruth, daughter of Thomas Wood; she was born July 21st in 1662; as a widow she married, October 26th 1696, John Lunt; she died November 29th, 1734.

Issue.

1. **Ruth Jewett,** born, Rowley, *circa* 1681; married October 3d 1697, Joseph Varnum, of Dracut.

2. **Joshua Jewett,** born in Ipswich, August 26th 1683; baptized same day; died October 15th 1694.

3. **Hannah Jewett,** born in Ipswich, April 3d 1685; baptized April 26th of the same year; died in Ipswich, November 23d 1685.

4. **Elizabeth Jewett,** twin of Hannah; baptized May 24th 1685; died in 1713.

5. **Joseph III Jewett,** baptized April 10th 1687; married, 1st, March 27th 1706, Mary Hibbert; her parentage is unknown; she died June 26th 1732, in her 43d year; 2dly, November 6th 1732, Mary, daughter of Rev. Edward Payson, minister of the church at Rowley, by Elizabeth Philips, his wife; she died January 22d 1748–49; he died August 10th 1747; left issue male.

6. **Sarah Jewett,** born February 3d 1688–89; baptized February 10th of the same year; married (published March 23d 1705–06) Samuel II Prime; she married 2dly, October 7th 1718 Robert Rogers; she died November 20th 1722.

7. **Priscilla Jewett,** baptized February 1st 1690–91; married February 2d 1708–09, Hilkiah Boynton, of Rowley.

8. **Johanna Jewett,** born April 12th 1693; baptized April 16th of the same year; married (published April 8th 1710) Jonathan Pickard of Rowley; she died July 26th 1748.

9. **Joshua Jewett,** born February 16th 1694–95; baptized the next day; married April 4th 1715, Mary, daughter of John Todd, of Rowley; he died October 30th 1760; left issue male.

Account of Joseph II Jewett.

On the Records he is styled: "Junior"; "Carpenter"; "Merchant", and in the last years of his life always "Captain." He lived for a short time in Ipswich.

Freeman July 9th 1684.

EDWARD JEWETT.

† 1616.

Maximillian Jewett.
† 1684;
left issue male.

Joseph I Jewett.
† 1661.

Jeremiah Jewett.
† 1714;
left issue male.

Nehemiah Jewett.
† 1720;
left issue male.

Joseph II Jewett.
† 1694.

Joseph III Jewett.
† 1747;
left issue male.

Sarah Jewett.
married 1st, Samuel I Prime,
2ndly, Robert Rogers.

Joshua Jewett.
† 1760;
left issue male.

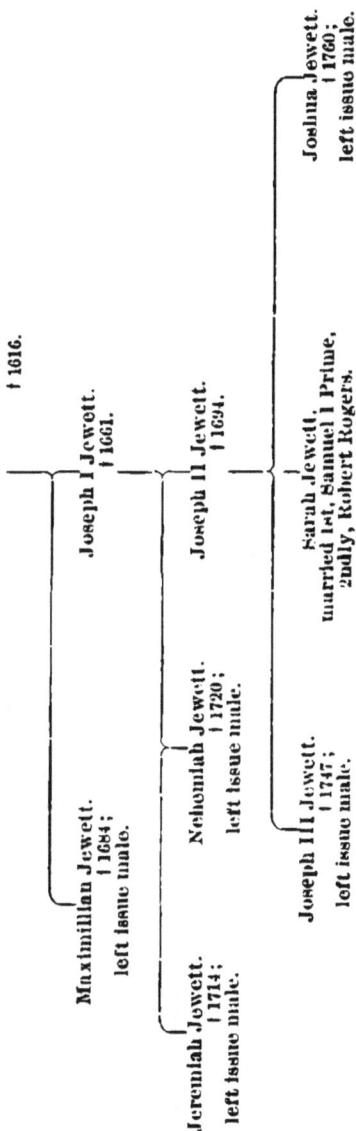

Will of Edward Jewet, of Bradford, West Riding of Yorkshire, England.[1]

In the name of God Amen the second day of February in the year of our Lord God 1614 in the XIjth year of the Reigne of our Sovereigne Lord James by the grace of God Kinge of England, France and Ireland defender of the faith etc. and of Scotland the eight and fortye whereas nothinge is more certaine then death and nothinge more uncertaine than the houre of death Therefore I Edward Jewet of Bradfud wth in the diocos of Yorke clothier though sicke and diseased in bodye yett sounde and fut in minde and memorye I praise God therefore doe in this uncertainty of life knowinge that even in health we are subject to death make publish and declare this my Last Will and testam^{t} in maner and forme followinge that is to say First and principally I give up and commend my soule in the hands of Almightye God my creator and redeemer hopeing and assuredly trusting to have full and free pardon and remission of all my sinnes by the p^{e}cious death and burial of Christ Jesus my alone Saviour and for jusstification by his righteousness and my bodye I yield to the earth to be decently buried at the discretion of my friends Item my will and minde is that all my lawfull debts be payde out of my whole goods. Item I give and bequeath two full parts of all my goods cattels chattels and credits in three parts to be divided unto William Jewet Maximilian Jewet Joseph Jewet and Sarah Jewet my children equally to be divided amongste them after my debts be paid and funerall expenses discharged. The third part and residue of all my said goods cattells chattels and credit I give and bequeath unto Mary my wife whome I make the sole executrix of this My Last Will and testament And I doe intreat William Taylor my father in law Henry Taylor my brother in law Samuel Taylor and Trustrum Ledgerd the supervisors of this my Last Will and

[1] Copied by Mr. H. G. Somerby, from the original in the Office of the Archdiocese at York.

Testam[t] Item my Will and minde is that my children shall have their porcons paide unto them at such times as they shall sevally accomplishe their ages of XXth yeares or otherwise lawfully demand the same Lastly I doe comitt the tucion and gov-mt of all my said children wt[h] theire severall porcons during theire severall minorities unto the said Mary my wife.

Will of Joseph I Jewett. (ESSEX INSTITUTE, HISTORICAL COLLECTIONS.)

I Joseph Jewett of Rowley beinge weake of boddy but perfect in understandinge and memory doe make this my last will and testament in manner and form as followeth, Imprimis after my debts beinge payed I desire the rest of my goods may bee equally divided among my seaven children, as well those two that I have by my last wyfe as the five that I had before. Allwayes provided that my oldest sonne Jeremiah Jewett must have a dubbel portion, of all estate I have both in New England, and Old, whether personall or Reall further provided that one hundred pounds I have allready payed to my sonne Phillip Nellson, that shall be counted as part of what I doe now give him, Item I doe give unto my sonne Jeremiah Jewett the farme I bought of Joseph Muzzy I meane all such Lands bought of him or any other, that are on the Norwest side of the River called Egipt River, with all the meadow I bought of Nathaniell Stow and Robert Lord Senior, provided he accept of it at five hundred pounds and whereas in the fourth line it is saide I desire the rest of my goods to be equally divided amongst my seaven children I meane Lands as well as goods and if any of those my above saide seaven children, should depart this life, before the age of twenty one yearse, or day of marriage then there portions, shall bee equally divided Amongst the rest, allwayes provided my eldest sonne Jeremiah shall have a doubell portion, and as for my two youngest children, and there portion I leave to the disposinge of my brother Maximillian Jewett, and who he shall apoint when he departeth this life, and I make Exequitors of this my last will and Testament my Brother Maximillian Jewett, and my sonne Phillip Nellson, my sonne John Carleton and my sonne Jeremiah Jewett Allwayes free and willinge that they shall be satisfied out of the estate, for all such pains and labour, that they shall be at concerning the above premisse.

Signed and sealed in the presence of us
EZEKIEL NORTHEND
MARK PRIME

JOSEPH JEWETT
Dated the 15 of february in the yeare 1660
At the signinge and sealinge hereof I doe give my Exequitors full power to make deeds and to confirme any Lands I have sold to any.
EZEKIEL NORTHEND MARKE PRIME

Bibliography.

New England Historical and Genealogical Register. Vol. VIII.

Essex Institute. Historical Collections. Vols. IV, V, VI, XIII, XIV, XV, XIX to XXIV.

History of Rowley, Mass., from 1639; with an address at the Second Centennial Anniversary by James Bradford. By Thomas Gage. Boston, 1840.

Genealogical Dictionary of the First Settlers of New England, by James Savage. Boston, 1860–62. 4 vols.

History of Sutton, Mass., 1704–1876; including Grafton until 1735; Millbury until 1813; and parts of Northbridge, Upton, and Auburn. By W. A. Benedict and H. A. Tracy. Worcester, 1878.

Annual Financial Report of the Town of Rowley. Rowley, 1893.

www.ingramcontent.com/pod-product-compliance
Lightning Source LLC
Chambersburg PA
CBHW020337090426
42735CB00009B/1574
* 9 7 8 3 7 4 3 4 1 3 4 8 1 *